PETE GREEN lives in Sheffield and s[...]
Their debut pamphlet *Sheffield Alma*[...]
are published by Longbarrow Press. [...]
full-length collection. Pete was short[...]
Prize in 2019 and longlisted in the N[...]
2020. As a musician and songwriter Pe[...]
Sweet Nothings and has released two solo albums, the more recent
being *We're Never Going Home* (Atomic Beat Records, 2016).

petegreensolo.com @petenothing

PETE GREEN
The Meanwhile Sites

CROMER

PUBLISHED BY SALT PUBLISHING 2022

2 4 6 8 10 9 7 5 3 1

First published in Great Britain in 2022 by
Salt Publishing Ltd
12 Norwich Road, Cromer, Norfolk NR27 0AX United Kingdom

www.saltpublishing.com

Salt Publishing Limited Reg. No. 5293401

A CIP catalogue record for this book is available from the British Library

ISBN 978 1 78463 269 4 (Paperback edition)

Typeset in Sabon by Salt Publishing

Printed and bound in Great Britain by Clays Ltd, Elcograf S.p.A

Contents

[1]

[11]

for Brian Lewis

[I]

Curlews

On a failing clifftop path
you halt and hush me,
pull out from the ice-flecked air
sad and steady minims
fluting through a perfect fifth.

This is their call. Curlews
glissando the headland
cluttered by gulls,
riding out the crisis
on soft thermals of aplomb.

Love, let's take some notes.

Every vanishing sparrow leaves
Delhi more unliveable

Every vanishing sparrow leaves Delhi more
unliveable. Developers favour panels tilting
air into domestic space. The dearth of ventilation
ducts spells nestlessness for house sparrows.
This drive for vaulted atriums is not the only
element. The thriving of blue rock pigeons
risks sparrows' viability. Moreover, automotive
factors swell the threat on several fronts.
Ravenous chirps of sparrow chicks go overwhelmed
by engines' din. Proliferating driveways veil
rich soils, starving the species out. Each absented
invertebrate leaves Delhi less invigorative.
Heavily enveloped in dioxins, downtown
spaces wane. Voided by a flock's departure,
sites renounce vivacity. This movement finds
the purview of the valuers of real estate.
The trade-off falls between biodiversity
and vanity. The benchmarks of convenience
versus *Passer domesticus*. Every vanquishing
player finds the spoils divide invalidly.
Chief minister Dikshit approved the sparrow
as Delhi's state bird. On Sanjay Van's periphery,
diasporas of sparrows sit. Every vanishing
sparrow leaves the city strangely vulnerable.

To a Vagrant Black-Throated Thrush Sighted in Grimsby Over Brexit Weekend

30 January 2020

Please display your plumage
with a neutral expression. The procedure

begins with these frontline officers
whose photography is vital to our records.

Sightings of your kind
are rare in this district. Any more than one

or two a year would represent
an influx and prompt policy reviews.

The sound shaking your feathers
is not incipient thunder but the ghosts

of boilermakers, trawlermen,
pumphouses by the graving dock,

fifty years of dereliction
now transmuted to a seismic growl.

Sing of the renegade currents
that jetstreamed you to this outpost,

picture to our colleagues
your undocumented passage of the Balkans,

your precarious flightpath
above Bohemia and Maastricht. Please

remain in the nest provided
for your own safety while your quarantine

is paperworked. Try not
to take flight, unnerved by the clicking shutters,

the gunpowder, the senior
rhubarb-hued men, their coronavirus glances,

the triumphalism spiked with envy,
the tripods morphing into pitchforks.

It is normal for your wings
to tremble at those explosions in the sky.

Dungeness

Perhaps we've come because
we are of the jetsam edged
out as England draws a bolt
across its garden gate,
where fruit withers
for want of a picker

and now the land's no longer
sectioned into row on row
of concrete yards,
high fences guarding
ranks of union jacks,
we've reached Dungeness:

ungovernable shingle
fashioned of splayed rope,
scrap steel plate, ramshackle
sheds, a mislaid trimaran;
unwalled gardens running
through an exclave of trust,

the offhand hum of fission
tossing out odd megawatts
to fuel a greater good,
counterpointed with
calciferous wash
of tide on worldly stone.

Perhaps we've come because
the driftwood used to joist
these unprotected homes
harbours stories from
each effusive port the sea
once showed it.

Love Song of Ingleton Road

This goes no further.
It's our spellbinding
brinkmanship that'll bring
us to this point together.

We are the town's final
stand. *Give way*, says the sign
where the grass starts to run
from prim to bacchanal

and this last run of terraced
houses narrows, like at the bar
in the Crown, when the men draw
in shoulders to let you past.

White noise from above—
a vaulted window amplifies
a shower: sound of a stylus
in a run-out groove.

This moment is our margin:
from the dusk your arms emerge,
straight as the map's edge.
When I was away I'd imagine

the white lines of the road
each time a train flashed past
to chorus our curbed wanderlust,
crumbling like stale bread.

The resolutely unexotic
minutes of our DNA unwinding
in the fading
scents of bitumen, static

and Ron's pipe tobacco;
then the run of smaller towns,
names pale grey like millstones,
receding like an echo.

Here's the fence panel
punched out by the storm
I heard about last autumn,
slates crashed in the ginnel

and houses yield to scrubland
where the horses browse
easy for a run to graze,
sufficient and unowned.

Sunset, then. Relief
from daylight's onus.
You reply *people like us*
aren't meant to "get on in life"

your sibilants lost in kissing
and the blue luminous blur,
yellow light, drum roll and roar
of the London train passing.

Dan of the Don

skitters the shallows
where the Sheaf interlopes,
waterboatman-sculptor
summoning splayed relic
stacks amid spate.

Dan's materials
parody permanence,
approximate props from the
lapsed pomp of
manufacture and shipment.

The half-built and derelict
timeshare Dan's habitat,
tributaries into the
current moment.
Dan's finished product

is our purblind straining
astride the meanders for
meaning, tracking an
implicit timeline,
positing vanishing points.

Dan of the Don knows well
the precarious weight
of all we inherit,
expresses the lot in teetering
stanzas of brick.

Postcard from a Staff Away Day

I'm writing this outside the Holiday Inn
while the coffee and the river flow. A fire
      escape, a plaque to commemorate
the station closed in 1970. My last boss
but one, the one I liked, stepped out to chat
and pointed out a platform's concrete lip.
      We riffed on how landscapes outlive
the reasons that reshape them, and the way
a dead-end viaduct, disremembered on a
city centre's undrawn boundary, becomes
      lonelier than anywhere.

Inside a hundred admin staff, marketers
and middle managers have broken off
      into small groups to stockpile
abstract nouns against austerity. This is now
      a time of great upheaval in the
landscape for our sector. Holding to our
values is the key to managing change.
      The posh facilitator once drove
round and round a roundabout in tears.
Her PowerPoint roadmapped the warning signs
      of unresolved transition.

Wish you were here. All that makes
sense today are the gold hypothetical
thread your steps narrate about the city
divining great upheaval in the landscape
      and the flicker of your eyes
as we watch decades tumble through a weir.

We would break off
for a listening process with the River Don,
    brainstorm with kingfishers,
    work in a pair to understand
our own responses to the changing
densenesses of reedbeds. We would
negotiate with dragonflies our action plan
    to leave things as they are.

The Absences

This scene. A playground in a suburb,
rainswept, nameless; a populace
implicit in the empty swing's
small restlessness. Here is Wednesday
afternoon. The path takes off

beyond drenched banks of
privet, flowerbeds clipped circular,
the glade above the cemetery
where Subway wrappers
missed the bin. Somewhere else

is where the soundtrack starts:
three streets away a builder's truck,
its empty flatbed's jolt and clank.
Assume its wipers' bland
defiance. On the adjacent corner

a salon's solitary client may
discreetly lick a fingertip
to riffle magazine pages,
yawning below the blowdry.
Her ringtone perhaps coincides

with the intervention of
a bell releasing scrums of pent-up
pupils and their performed bluster.
Headlights will sweep
the first shadings of dusk

but all of that is elsewhere
and to come. Instead zoom in—
a poplar leaf relinquishes
a single droplet with the seasoned
hand of a Speyside connoisseur

which slaloms down the frame
cradling the swings, negotiates
angular graffiti scratched into the
decades, each layer a trend, a rise
and fall, a sea-change, a regime.

Three tanka from Staithes

This busy half-hour—
a heron has come and gone,
gauzy fog grown dense,
rising tide of afternoon
gained an inch against my boot

*

On the darkened beach,
lamplight from a single room
in a bungalow
cut loose on the clifftop's fold
reaches down to us like stars

*

All I know is that
driftwood lifted from the sand
to burn in the stove
of our borrowed cottage is
the crowning of all my poems

Far North Line

When I go north I learn of scale, of continuity.
There's always further left to go. A saltire
whips above a shed, like a five-bar gate swinging
open in a storm. This is Brora: scantness,
dauntless, a moment of the world

leaning in. Trampoline children hang
in the air, grin at the train, spread fingertips scribing
curves through sparse atmosphere.
One grey, folded man counts
down days from a speck of a bungalow.

This line's an exercise, this trip a practice of
absurd immersions. Emptiness is
exponential. "How are we going to get back?"
you beam, necking more Jura. A perching heron
pleases you. A girl is old enough

to graze a horse alone by breaking waves,
young enough to wave up
at our approach to Helmsdale. Somewhere
it's Saturday afternoon, somewhere
our kids scoff cake. Forty miles more of Caithness

emptiness await. How are we going to get back?

Ring of Brodgar

August 2015

We crouch away in Orkney, turn
faces from the mainland's turbulence,
a nation fracturing from stress.
They'll never notice if we set up home

beyond the Ring of Brodgar,
dodge the draft, as if the miles
between our pulse and London will
suffice, as if somehow

the stones won't let us starve.
What faith is this? It's not
that of the new-age types who
talk all mystical, tell us they sense

some twitch of atavistic energy
when the elongated shadows
of a solstice dawn touch henges.
This creed is purchaseless. We're too

far gone. If there's some distant
essence inside us, sending pulses out
to seek electric resonance
with the Earth's magnetic soul, it's

routed in our ravaging
by light pollution, trending topics,
sat nav. We are stardust. We are tarmac,
raddled as caffeine-stoked receptionists

overdoing sunbeds. We are a king's
remains interred below parked cars.
And look at how we place cold
palms upon the cold

face of the uprights, embrace these
seven types of sandstone
instinctively as if we scratch an itch,
expect to feel something. But look at how

it's been here all along. Consider
how the ring was seen between
the fadeout of its Neolithic meaning
and the modern age,

the way a focal point became
a backdrop, unconsidered,
the layering of complacency
like strata of silt—

across at Skara Brae
it took a savage storm
to eradicate that murk.
Let us celebrate

unironically
enlightenment's sufficient might
to exacavate this circle
from indifference.

The Old Man of Hoy

So
reimagine
that sixties dictum
casting Warhol as a
sea-stack: everyone's
famous for fifteen
centuries. I'll give them
old. The cheeky sods.
Mine will be the sweet
and fitting doom of a
Romantic in his prime:
Shelley lost foreseeing
his own watery demise.
Mine will be a final act of
the grandeur you'd expect
of a leading Orcadian rock star.
For now, check out my fans:
geologically a prodigy, I'll
strike a neolithic pose, pouting
as they Instagram my strata,
sandstone red and splendid
in reposed Atlantic sun. Old?
Take your pick. For the instant
of your cameraphone's ersatz
click,
I'm Monroe, I'm Tom Chatterton,
Princess Di and Richey Manic.
You know what they say:
live palaeolithically fast,
die young. When my bones

batter the basalt beneath me,
  I'll leave 'em wanting more,
  flocking for the ferry trip that takes
in my tumultuous finale. Watch the
touts flog tickets for ten times their
  face value. I've always said I'll make
a big splash. Better to shatter
and spectacularly part the waves,
  felled by a fifty-foot crack in your south
face splitting like Hendrix's star-
                    spangled banner
  to take on board the furious spume, the
                    surf of ages
than erode away. I'll finish on a song.

Leaving Stromness

The gneissic grey of the stone
                             buildings that huddle the
harbour like gathered relatives
                          is the grey of Scapa Flow,
the grey of the gunmetal
                    battle fleet scuppered below,
scuttled as von Reuter got
                       the wrong end of the stick;
the grey spread of the meanings
                      strewn between intent
and sense received,
               the grey of the neolithic
                    matter, the unweathered
rock of the dwellings of Skara Brae,
                       the enigma of all endings.
And today
             the grey exhaust of the
                     Kirkwall airport bus asserting
motion into this mild late summer
                  is the grey between the doubtless
black of our imminent
                   mortgaged mainland,
                       tomorrow's admin meetings
and the white of the cloud
                    swilling from the cliffs of Hoy
like froth off last night's lively IPA
                  the extravagant white of this
surprise of mist ghosting up
                off Hoy Sound now, intoning

what, you're leaving now? We're
                              just getting started, stay
        for one more drink, one more
                              surprise
                              for the road.

The Pull

Carlisle's air felt charged, like air
above a waterfall. The football
caterwauls that flared across
the forecourt resonated more
raucous for the latitude,
as if the North's high magnetism
played acoustic engineer,
aligning ions, optimising
ozone for full reverb. That's
some atmosphere.

          So I drove on
for Glasgow, Oslo, heard a Nordic
echo of my Humber uncles,
men who called the children *bains*,
forefathered by Danes dispersed in
longboats to the North Sea's margins.
Sensing the diaspora,
my prompted blood obeyed the pull.

I saw three ships. In a museum,
unearthed by farmers. Eerily
unravaged by the centuries
of tarry ooze that interposed
over their Viking burials, these
vessels for the afterlife
yet decomposed in air,
the fabric of their clinkered oak
unravelling an atom at a
time. Each archaeologist

kills the thing he loves. Three ships,
dissolved by their own salvaging.

I saw three more, bound to disburse
cargoes of containered iron,
concrete, paper, grain, and salt
beneath a sky conveying carbon.
Dusk and ships between them held
the stuff of life.

                    A fleet of trucks
hauled off the goods, exporting photons
from their headlamps to the glassy
tabletop of Oslofjord,
this school of jiving lights a spectral
replica of Gardermoen's
runway. I was riveted.

I set my sights on Thurso, Tromsø,
heard my hosts share theories
of light and sociability. Far
north, they said, the tilted Earth
and prismed hours will put a slant
on how folk are. They will mark down
the southern inclination to
elliptical. They will decline
to take water with whisky, they
will tend toward the festival,
the lantern; sagas; firesides.

So, one ship more. The hull of Fram
was as a hazelnut: so smoothed and
rounded that the polar ice's
pulverising grip would merely
slide below the boards. Drawn in,
my office-worker fingers played
across the nameplate on the door
of Amundsen's Antarctic cabin,
visitor. And nervous flyer.
Yet the pull that once compelled
Nansen, Franklin, Amundsen
ripples to the sandwich-nibbling
salarymen of Skipton, Swindon,
logging on to trace the paths
of satellites across pack ice,
pixellated glacial plains,
terra incognita by the
terabyte.

       The polar pull
makes irony of iron will.
Blood tautens with a ferric prickle
to the pole's imperative.

If Anything Happens To Me

Before this seaborne escapade
the lad who put his seed in me
issued reassurances. Sweet of him.
He didn't need to. Premiums
are out of reach, but some
makeshift scheme's in place.
Love, he says, *I've had a word.*
The lads'd see you right.
You and the bain'd not starve.

He's installed an app so I can
track their trawler on the waves
when I wake for night feeds, though
the signal from the monitor
won't quite carry baby cries
to the Dogger Bank.

His mam's beside herself.
The toughest job there is, say folk
who've only had one job.
I know. It's treacherous
and every family knows a lad
come back from sea with
half his arm pulped in the winch
or who's not come back.

I waved him off and grimaced: *well,*
mortgage won't pay itself
and didn't tell him how
at playgroup they want to know

when do you return to work,
how I just laugh. Nor did I add:

if there's a cage, at least let it be
gilded. Or: *I wish to Christ*
something would
happen to me.

The Money Tree

Up the track from Grindleford, our boots
crack through zesty bracken, nettle, lichen,

thread between strewn millstones,
haphazard, weathered, pockmarked

as the moon, emerald-edged with mosses,
spilt like change fumbled from

the pocket of a careless century.
This is the Longshaw Estate, bought

in 1928 by the people of Sheffield,
held in trust for the pleasure of all.

We talk about your nursery
in its final months of life

and how the library might be next.
Here's the money tree.

In their fortieth month of life
your apricot-soft hands grip and spread

across the rasping surface of a stone,
strike small change between the gaping

fibres of rain-tendered timber,
smacking down the queen.

Wet chips of the stone scatter,
the stone soft after all.

Don't tell me your wish.

[11]

Pulp

1. WASTE

The creased and brown-speckled beermat that you kept
    from that first faltering drink in the White Lion.
The two pencilled copies of the short fiction omnibus
    from the modernism module where you met.
The Bible with those verses from Hebrews underlined
    concerning hospitality to strangers and angels.
The flyer detailing the tree protests which your boss
    carried in to the office specifically to dismiss.

The maple and walnut chessboard opened at Christmas
    where Jack will checkmate you on Whit Sunday.
The ornate *tamburica* you will eventually learn to play
    though never with your dad's silken adeptness.
The election leaflet today promoting your deportation.
    The queenly pink certificate that keeps you put.
The tidied allotment shed where he told you the tumour
    would apparently be inoperable at this late stage.

The compact plywood box that saves your train tickets
    in lieu of a diary. All of your saved train tickets.
The order of service from before you dispersed the ashes
    in the wood with incongruous wristy flourishes.
The derelict dolls' house lined with maroon wax crayon
    which was Sophie's, then Jack's, then no-one's.
The huge doors of Carnegie's bar squeaking like a fiddle
    at the wake. All these things are made of the trees.

You, Sophie and Jack. Your late-blossoming curiosity
about folk music and kayaking. The ashy texture
of your greying hair. The cold air in your lungs right now
as you wonder if anyone else will ever remember
the console in the old library with square coloured lights
and a sleek zinc slot where they punched the card
which looked like a thing from *Blake's 7*. The faltering.
The trees. All these things are made of your dad.

2. THE FLYER

From his doormat he lifts a flyer
about a protest to save the trees

on a street in the adjacent suburb.
It stresses the iconic status of the trees,

planted to honour local war dead
a century ago, as well as the trees'

ecological usefulness, quantifying
the carbon absorbed by mature trees.

The text discusses property values
and the aesthetic appeal of trees,

finally demanding a root and branch review
of the council's policy on street trees.

He scans the content while looking
through the bay window at the trees

above his new Octavia hatchback.
The flyer names specific trees,

plane and sycamore, and he is amused
to find himself fancying that the trees

are people he knows. That sprawling
beech down the hill where the trees

wreck pavements is his pyjama-wrapped,
stroke-wracked dad. Three odd-sized trees

edging the park are George from work
with two prodigious kids; silver birch trees

his poised PA in plaid skirt. Spring is here
and the birds have returned to the trees

and his new Octavia hatchback
will need to be washed. *Save the trees*?

he will say at the dinner table later,
waving the flyer toward the trees,

noting that the flyer is made from paper
and that paper is made from trees.

He will genuinely believe
himself to be as sharp as any axe.

There is no slack in the system. There are no coal mines
    but those minutes your Sophie spent
    painting a canary-yellow elephant
could have been employed usefully. Think not of means

but ends. There is so much pressure to be competitive.
    The nation needs Apple pioneers,
    search engineers, cashless cashiers,
black marketeers, forced volunteers. If we are to thrive

then Sophie's undoubted creativity must become a force
    for future growth. If she has dreams,
    let them be of parkour meeting rooms,
pop-up unicycle megastores and milk-free cereal cafés,

edgy burger joints themed after Balkan warlords,
    how to brand a gangsta letting agency.
    We must weigh every contingency
the terms and tariffs might throw at us. Imagine loads

on pallets in warehouses stacked high with adverbials
    and nobody to front them; or a field
    where adverbial crops have not failed
but rot, unfronted, on the stalk. These kinds of skills

are key to our recovery. Here's a useful mental image:
             it may help to think of Sophie's mind
             as the global trade war's battleground
and as we know, every war inflicts collateral damage.

You learned to draw shapes on a mono green screen
             by programming in LOGO. I learned
             technical drawing. We have since turned
our hands to advanced conference venue facilitation,

the management of management, the outsourcing
             of outsourcing plans to specialist
             metaconsultancies. Causes of waste
or inefficiency will be eliminated. You are facing

up to our responsibilities, among which: not to fiddle
             while the Square Mile burns. Before
             music was rationalised, you'll be aware,
came Sophie's infamous trance episode: violin bow idle

across her thighs, vacant stare. Obviously neither
             of us wants to see a repeat. No slack
             in the system, no free ride, no tea break
culture, no white space. We are all in this together.

4. LOCK-IN AT CARNEGIE'S

Midnight came and went and the masses downed
their pints of Baudelaire porter,
set brown-foamed glasses on beermats of recycled
encyclopaedia, and returned
to darkness. Black-clad cognoscenti have exchanged
glances laced with meaning, nursing
dregs of Guinness, drops of cognac. Now, half-moon
bespectacled, auspicious
in fluent velvet cardigan, the landlady ceremonially
lifts from around the neck of a snowy owl
a hefty but intricately detailed brass key
on a crimson taffeta sash.
Majestic in gait, she crosses the room, applies a twist
to the key, securing double oak doors
against the embers of night. Shutters carved
with vine motifs and scrolls
rotate to black out steamed and leaking windows,
erase the street lights of South Road.
Bar staff go among the tables, set down pencils,
notepaper. The lights fall low.
Walls revolve, reveal banks of bookcases unseen
since the joint converted. Deprived
eyes fall on spines and titles, lap up possibilities.
A tenor sax fugues jazz.
Thirsting for print, the guests make for the shelves,
furtiveness half-forgotten, seizing
on samizdat anthologies, a transgressive history
of needlecraft, the atlases

they only heard rumours of. A rhythm section joins
the sax, easy, effortless. The landlady beams
like the full moon, idly fondling a date stamp.
Warm rain adds percussion.
Millennials with MacBooks sample artisan unfiltered
wi-fi, craft the beermats into bookmarks,
gossip of plagiarism and publishing house mergers.
Quick-witted Jack flits
from first floor vantage point to the back stairs
then the counter, junior binoculars in hand,
whispers to the landlady with urgency. Crisis is afoot.
Sssshhhhhhhh!
hisses the landlady, secretly enjoying it. The band
stops. Heavy knocking through the oak.
Readers scurry to conceal books. Bookcases recede
into the walls again,
the stony mechanism grinding through the floor
as the knocking gathers urgency and ire.
Agents from the licensing authority have heard
reports that the premises
have illicitly reverted to their previous function
and are obliged to investigate potential
unauthorised exchanges of printed or digital material
in a public building.
All seems, at first, to be in order; then, a fumbling
in the room's far corner. One maladroit
punter struggles to put away a new *Practical Mechanic*.
The lit feds cross the floor.
The sergeant pushes forth a nightstick, pins open
the magazine. All of Carnegie's swallows

hard. The sergeant clicks his fingers and his men
        set about the room.
              Within a minute they locate the levers, lay bare
    clandestine literatures case by case by case,
rifle through all rucksacks, seize on volumes,
        faces ever grimmer.
            All gazes fix the counter where the sergeant
    now eyeballs the unflinching landlady,
his jackboot compressing *A Brief History of Time*.
    The moment distends.
           After a small eternity he asks if they have the new
    Sean O'Brien collection, as he's heard
O'Brien's back on form. A pause. A broad grin bursts
        across the sergeant's face.
           Laughter seizes the landlady. The lights dip again,
    the musicians blast Louisiana zydeco,
joined by a colliery brass band. Rain shimmies
        down the window frames.
           The licensing agents browse Chandler and Christie;
    sergeant and landlady jive, her cardigan
shimmering in candlelight. Jack earns an hour
        in the YA fiction section,
            chooses several titles slightly too old for him.
    Get stewed, laughs the studious postgraduate
in Philip Larkin specs who's barely uttered
        a word all night,
           Books are tomorrow's biofuel! Nobody knows
    what he means, but the crowd cheers anyway
just as the band changes key from G to A.
        The round he buys

for everyone begins with a Li Po lychee wine,
an Under Milk Wood bible-black lactose IPA,
a double Southern Comfort with ice and lime and
a mixer of Yorkshire rain.

5. UTILITY

after Wilfred Owen

Stack the trunks in the sun—
Gently its touch nurtured them once,
Summoned pale saplings to mourn
Pale boys-next-door dispatched to France,
The wide century's innocence lost
Where they were felled. So, go protest
The mechanisms that lay waste;

Conceive, in turn, new embryos
To honour those sacrificed sycamores,
The ribbons' time-stained yellows
Affirming the fertility of wars—
Or better yet, spurn rationale
To balance books, audit the soil;
Or germinate no seed at all.

Acton

August 2019

At least the breeze might roam
between high-rise and low
or beyond the estates

sequenced like chapters,
residents as old
as the walls are young.

Modest basslines ripple
between container walls
in Hope Gardens' courtyard

while the fathers
Uber gap-year Texans
over Tower Bridge and back.

This Sunday afternoon
place and moment
grow coterminous

while the breeze
rousing these hazels
weighs up its next move.

The Meanwhile Sites

The festival site on the Monday
where unfelt sunlight plays on speaker stacks,

ostensibly silent. How long can reverberations
from the encore's culminating chord persist

and what will succeed the meanwhile
sites of our small wins? Here's where we

spoke of distanced parents, here's where we danced
with Claire for an hour fifteen without a break,

shedding the dead weight of limits, forgetting
the weekend's long insistence on rain.

Presumably at some point we will not be beautiful,
cracks having crossed Claire's face and weeds

sprouted from the space between the beats
of my misfiring heart. Every half-hour we rise

to mute the radio news, its slow rock-steady
riff of depletion and winding-up. DJ, play a song

from before the sub-prime mortgage crisis.
How long can reverberations persist,

how many more seasons until
breaking sunlight doesn't wait for Monday.

Millennials

Millennials work in Starbucks and will never have children.
Take care around millennials. Their life expectations
May differ radically from your own. If you encounter one
Keep a pension plan and a cliché within reach. Millennials
May not regard a career as the noblest human aspiration,
In response to the imminent expiration of the career
As a thing. Millennials are digital natives. Many live-tweet
Their own birth. They may display little interest
In their local newspaper reporting a custard shortage
And be unfamiliar with procedures in the House of Lords.
To escape detection, millennials cunningly
Do not refer to themselves as millennials. They tend
To confuse their pursuers by releasing a stream of irony,
Or tears. Millennials' enemies are the Gen X-ers,
They engage in notorious battles on Brighton beach.
Millennials buy from small independent shops,
And large chain stores in malls, and sometimes
Retailers of medium size. Millennials have been known
To take care over their appearance, and sometimes
Not to. Though they will never own them, millennials
Almost always live in flats and houses. New millennials
Are entering the marketplace every year. Be vigilant.
Experts say millennials may appear in human form.

Amber

Amber joins me on the walk to work.
She points out how

in winter, butter-coloured
skies like these

anticipate the sun
before it's fully risen

like an airport decked in flags,
resplendent

before a monarch disembarks.
Amber loves to see

the Arts Tower in silhouette—
we know that post-war

hopefulness had long gone
when we joined the world,

dissipated like a wave on sand,
but still.

It's Sheffield's own Atomium,
she says: our monument to optimism

as the 52 roars past.
Amber glimpses someone's open

paperback, a passenger's,
and speculates about the words,

dashing off a smart haiku
while she paints her nails gold.

A driver grinds his gears while
waiting for the lights

to change. You saw that tweet—
Poets, we get it. Things

are like other things
and Amber spots a friend from school,

first time in more than 20 years.
Everyone's

a metaphor for someone else
and Amber's got an early date

about her unpaid JSA
somewhere over Burngreave way.

Rigid at my desk,
the day set

with the scrolling spreadsheet's
empty cells,

I muse on those Jurassic flies
secured in sap and fossilised

and then I realise
Amber isn't crying.

To a Person Employed to Stand on the University Roundabout at the Evening Rush Hour Holding a Large Advertisement for Domino's Pizza

And when the sixth hour was come
and Windows was shutting down
there was darkness over
              the whole land.

For a moment I believed
you were crossing Western Bank
but you are nailed to the spot
to proclaim this good news.
I rejoice in your gospel. I will
buy one get one free,
while the meek will inherit
the bus, the washing-up.
Saviour of the populace,
stigmatised, you feed the five
hundred thousand—age of modern
miracles made flesh. *Anno domini.*

        We are one with you
and you with us: ingesting the city—
with each monoxide breath
your life a little shortened
              for our sins.
Father, forgive them
pepperoni, twisted doughballs—
O the medium is the message,
              thus
I eat your flesh and drink your blood,

                    buy into your
blackened lung. We're all of us
            dying inside.

The Scorched Earth Masquerade Ball

The chimney hails us with a slimmer plume.
Circumstances this year being diminished
our unseen hosts can only heat the ballroom.
Thirty unseen chambers recede into disuse,
reeling outposts of an empire done and finished.
This is the Scorched Earth Masquerade Ball.
The doorman declines to greet and introduce
the guests, tosses lateral flow tests in the trash,
accrues and monetises data from our footfall,
smoothing down his Chemical Ali moustache.
We arrive just as the pinot noir is poured
onto the flames. We always have. The theft
we couldn't stop, the homes we can't afford,
the avocado narratives. It's all of our faults.
Nowhere left, we sing, *there's nowhere left
to go.* The innovations of Tomorrow's World
bought and placed to moulder in the vaults
below the hall. Guests are spun and twirled
Northern Soul-style round a long dancefloor
powdered with detritus from the crumbling
balustrades, or moon rock. By a parallel door
the Phantom of the Opera enumerates Apollo
astronauts still living. An heiress is stumbling
over her words and Theresa May kitten heels
as between clauses she pauses to swallow
prosecco and echo the room's big reveals
regarding the mother of all parties. The band
plays Blue Monday on a theremin and saw,
banjo and stand-up bass. *Have you planned
your retirement?* miaows the lead singer.

A flock of black doves flutter from her paw.
This is the Scorched Earth Masquerade Ball.
The servers of drinks are all a dead ringer
for Old Father Time or the Emir of Kuwait.
In the shadows around the far end of the hall
a flock of freelance watercolourists illustrate
a scene of brake lights through exhaust gas.
Our advances are plot spoilers and memes,
the motto of our team *all things must pass*
and our signature tune is the word *already*,
hit singles lost in disremembered dreams,
the final fade of Mr Blue Sky's robot voice,
the boards below us brittle and unsteady.
As good as it got. All the ball guests know
in tired veins the last leaseholders' choice
to run the well to dry exhaustion and bestow
a grand inheritance of nowhere left to go,
Houston, there's nowhere left to go. We've
heard the chimes at midnight on YouTube.
To mark the moment all the guests receive
the sacramental passing of a zinc hip flask
charged with crude oil and a calved-off cube
of Antarctic ice. Now to remove the mask
the guests throw gestures, synchronised. All
bear facial birthmarks shaped exactly like
the Persian Gulf. A grand embarrassed cough.
This is the Scorched Earth Masquerade Ball.
These are the zero hours. A massive airstrike
or a snap election will suffice to see us off.

Cold

Yes. I remember cold. You can write that down.
I will tell you everything. My archive brims
with classified accounts of frost more precise
than the confessions of all other clients,
their stilted talk of whites and callous blues.
Has it been so long? Your turquoise eyes
widen. I could gift you the quicksilver glint
of writhing herring or a breath's brief angel-wing
shimmer condensing in airborne iotas of ice
but blue is not feeling the recovery plan.

Yes, I remember cold. No-one is listening.
I will tell you everything. I will tell you
of the arrowhead of swifts flitting to winter
in distant continents, the midnight glockenspiel
two streets away, the absolute rigidity
of hexagons, the neon splay of striplights
across naked platform tarmac in some shuttered
factory suburb which the last train's given up on.
You can feel it just by thinking it. Dispense
with my heresy via the necessary processes
and you will have to redact the ill-suppressed
flinch that flared across your glassy visage
back there. Your complicity will keep me warm
tonight. Did we overstep a mark? Did someone
                    just walk over your grave?

They have dressed the terror barricades
like Christmas presents

They have dressed the terror barricades like Christmas presents.
Devout antivaxxers or zealous incels aspiring to plough the fields
of shoppers will be thwarted with a festive twist. Patient as reindeer
round the calendar, these rows of concrete blocks sleep unadorned
awaiting the scenario. Their moment in the snow. Something
in their straightforward perpendiculars bespeaks the optimism
of the architect urging the nation forward after war. Semiautomatic
high-vis cops pace high streets, firearms expectant as stockings
at midnight. A primed child looks up. Ho ho ho have you been good
are you ready for Christmas. They have dressed the terror barricades
like presents. This is where we live now. The SUV that some extremist
would deploy to strew our limbs among giftwrap and Argos bags
will instead end wrapped around a cheerful scarlet package
the size of your dinner table, trimmed with golden ribbons. Orphaned
strands of tinsel will find your eye from a mud-choked gutter
on your first commute of the new year. You will feel the lightless
treeless sitting room to be emptier than November's and you will
know terror at 4 in the afternoon in the weight of darkness falling.

The Value of Your Investments May Go Down as Well as Up

Your home may be at risk if you do not dream of drainage.
Water rising overnight may permeate stamp collections.
Your policy may not equate to a sandbag.

Flocks of surveyors may come to rest on local reedbeds.
The floodplain's tangible market price may differ from their valuation.
Your waterfront view may be affected.

Decommissioned brooks may rise again without prior notification.
Your rockery or wicker furniture may be affected.
You may choose to sleep in wellingtons.

Branches of the willow may be franchised to various operators.
Tolls may be imposed upon the third and second stepping stones.
Apologies for any inconvenience will follow.

The river's lease may pass to futures traders on the Taipei stock exchange.
No deity may be held responsible for Acts of God.
Prayer does not constitute a contract in law.

Men may arrive in hi-vis vests over pressed suits and blue-grey ties.
Your pension may be at risk if you do not seal your keyhole.
The liquidity of your assets is anyone's guess.

Outflow from damaged mains may pass directly to wastepipes.
Clauses may pass directly from the printer to the wastebasket.
Efforts have been made to ensure that systems are watertight.

Gated communities at dusk may know the game is up.
Taking off to roost, crows may cross a foreclosed drainage ditch.
Your heart's ease may be affected.

In the end there may realistically be very little you can do.
The conclusions of the report may resound like a zinc alloy gong.
You may find there is no collective noun for economists.

My heart is not iambic

My heart is not iambic
My heart was reverse engineered from a mapping by
transthoracic echocardiogram, yielding the blueprints
for sonic cathedrals
My heart is not iambic, nor spondaic, nor the pedestrian
drummer who plods the terrains of mid-tempo with a
landfill indie band
My heart is sometimes dactylic with episodes of paroxysmal
sprung rhythm
My heart improvises interludes in awkward times, 5/4, 9/8
My heart knows the grand insurmountable force of the notes
you don't play, of the beats that it skips, of white space
on a page, of mutual deterrence
My heart is a concept album about brinkmanship
My heart tends to improvise lengthy meandering solos
remembering kisses averted by ice-cool disposal squads
snipping through the correct artery with three seconds
remaining on the timer
My heart still extrapolates four hypothetical lovers from out
of the time-effaced memory of those averted kisses
My heart has a GPS tracker which faithfully relays its roving
data to my hypothetical lovers
My heart is revealed by the tracker at moments of orgasm,
D chord, and total eclipse to be located simultaneously
everywhere and nowhere
My heart is awaiting the leaving of my hypothetical
lovers, allowing its status to switch to unknown,
simultaneously beating and not beating
My heart is Schrödinger's heart
My heart did not chart

My heart is the makeshift device that failed to detonate but
      is yet to be made safe

My heart is not iambic

My heart's frequent flare-ups of narrow complex tachycardia
      aim to articulate some of the many anxieties of a
      fibrillating world

My heart notes the way Ernest Rutherford's work split the
      atom and aims to apply the same principles to itself, to
      your name, to common sense, to split the morpheme

My heart's diffident rhythm is fixed by the faltering tick
      of the dissident bomb that forgot the script and
      slumbered forlorn in an Audi Coupé during my
      blowout in a bar 50 metres away

My heart's twitchy syncopation is chiefly dictated by Article
      50 and Hurricane Katrina

My heart rate reflects fluctuations in staffing of libraries and
      the declining extent of polar bear territory

My heart takes the point that unemphasised syllables echo
      the stressed beats to come but sinkholes in Florida
      issue no terse coded warning before ingesting a
      laundromat

My heart rejects regular metre and classic fixed forms on the
      basis that both constitute a poetic and cardiological
      fallacy during a week that sees mustard gas cascade on
      Damascus and the Duchess of Sussex close a car door

My heart may have once been iambic but not since it marked
      the chaotic dispersion of billowing rubble and dust
      from the asymmetrical collapse of the towers

My heart acts on feedback from specialists finding no special
    affinity threading a rock-steady narrative *ba-dum
    ba-dum ba-dum* through a midnight flurry of knives in
    backstreet Hackney
My heart has been scanned under sterile conditions by
    prominent figures in cultural studies and diagnosed as
    post-ironic with high risk of becoming post-post-ironic

My heart is not iambic
My heart was once schooled in strict rhyming tetrameter
    pairs by a time-serving teacher detesting all poetry,
    children or both, and predictably it took a wayward
    turn
My heart pauses frequently, giving your heart ample
    time to confirm understanding or challenge the
    presuppositions underlying its most recent beat
My heart is the one who asks unneeded questions as
    seminars draw to a close, thus incurring the fury of
    delegates by delaying the break for coffee
My heart has no integral memory and strongly objects to the
    use of the phrase 'off by heart' to denote something
    learned
My heart is the opposite of autocorrect
My heart is an obsolete means of encryption
My heart is making landfall over Gulfport, Mississippi
My heart suspends its business so that summits can conclude
    negotiations and sign off important treaties between
    beats
My heart looked on passively as the space between its beats
    was declared *terra nullius* by a speculative group of

internet cranks who proceeded to colonise the space
and found a micronation
My heart then evicted the settlers by beating at 149 bpm
My heart leaves its beating to one day before a tough
deadline and then pulls an all-nighter
My heart is not teetotal
My heart is basically trolling me
My heart is appalled by its own timidity
My heart's staccato signature is as distinctive as a fingerprint
and will betray me to the authorities
My heart's latest plot was uncovered by squads of elite
cardiologists fixing electrodes to my trembling skin
and monitoring its suspicious activity for 48 hours
When they flicked a switch the screen montaged through
ones and zeroes, nanobots, flash floods, tap water run
through with trihalomethanes and lead, convulsing
commodity markets, the planet's dwindling lithium
deposits, zeroes, trenches of flame stacked with
oranges covered in kerosene then set ablaze to
protect wholesale value, ones and zeroes, a soundless
Nuremberg rally with a million blank faces in
headphones, zeroes, barcode tattoos, 3D-printed
handguns, a human resources boss contemplating
subcutaneous microchip implants to monitor staff,
flatlining commodity markets, quantum foam, grey
goo, the whole world swiping left

[III]

I am the king of Belgium

I am the king of Belgium. See me patronise
la Grand-Place, my regal smile
beneficent among allies

disgorging from the Eurostar
on diplomatic business
to locate our finest lambic bar.

Sure, you may regard a grander square
or two in Prague, Madrid,
New York. Well, don't compare—

just mark the gilded light that baffles
this thin drizzle, glancing off the corniced
guildhalls, mild as cream on waffles.

In French this house is mine:
Maison du roi. In Dutch, the *Broodhuis*—
breadhouse. Both are fine

but Americans express surprise
to see my royal highness stand
and guzzle *frites* with mayonnaise.

I am the king of Belgium, and with me
the k in *king* stays lower case.
We don't stand on orthography

round here—though we have sent
well-drafted memorandums of support
to the nascent government

at Holyrood. Perfectly formed,
my realm is central to our continent.
Here is no Bastille to be stormed,

just a modest parliament, gothic town hall,
chocolatiers, cherry beers, dozing
scarlet dahlias strung along a stall:

a capital whose name distressed
Englishmen invoke to flag their scripted fears.
That island lying due northwest

reserves itself—but from this spot the tracks
to Europe's endpoints radiate
just like the spokes of union jacks.

I am of a class that likes an agile domain,
fleet-footed in a time that sees
the superpowers on the wane:

we are the kings of Belgium and of Zeeland,
the emperor of Luxembourg,
the tzars of Zetland, Shetland, Sealand.

That's how we get along—
and so back on the *Place* I pace
unnoticed through the throng,

black Converse below my robes. That's all:
a monarch for an age disrobed of grandeur.
I am the king of Belgium. Think small.

Holding Out

We've made a makeshift dormitory of Pete's through-
lounge. This wasted distribution of limbs and duvets
suggests some aftermath—debauchery? disaster? That
was some night we just had. Downstairs from the show
one-time colliers stood on, to nurse bemusement with a
dark brown pint. It's the glitter on our faces, now the
ringing in our ears. It's mercury in our artery: fleet-foot-
edness, slow poison.

Or it's the impossible nature of the enterprise. Brooklyn
accents borne across a venue purpose-built for other
things; a bassist from Kyoto in an A-line tartan skirt,
in the bingo caller's place. In duffel coats and plastic
beads we're somewhere on a scale between stoutness
and denial, curfew holding no more sway than fashion.
Her power cut, the singer caterwauled unto a nosebleed.

Hours and miles from now we'll blink away this beatific
jetlag, as if Emma's 8-bit synthtone and its stories haven't
stripped us down like clapped-out engines, reconditioned
us, purring and permanently changed. We'll resume the
motions of responsibility, the school run, the washing of
faces, back in our own cities to perform the languid dice-
roll of the 9 to 5 with our superiors: voracious champions
at the game whose rules they make.

And this time they'll be furious at how we ride on
through untouched, still stardust-girded from this show,
this aftermath, impervious, the ludicrousness of it all laid
bare by those neon overdriven chords and synchronicity

and the love—I'll call it love—strung out like a paper-chain or coda between the line of mattresses I glance along, between the fall of strategems to banish wake-fulness.

Now this phone is flashing up a Wiki page about those soldiers holed up in the forests, hostilities long having ceased: the last was Private Nakamura, found on Morotai in 1974. Now a toss and snore from the drummer I shared whisky and vegan brownies with. This is something more complex than bare subsistence; but perhaps one day the authorities will fetch us back, honour us, and do their best to settle every one of us back into society.

Postcard from the 1970s

Charging my iPhone 11 is an interesting challenge
and I can't get veggie bacon for love nor money
but when the train's privatised livery reverted
to indigo and grey and I alighted into the 70s
I felt a notification vibrate in my vagabond heart.
So much violence. So much naivety. Here nothing
is weightless, no touchscreen lightness marks
the way they interface with tech. So much substance:
from the lumbering bulk of a brutalist precinct
to the bash of a mutton chop on a butcher's
marble block, or the supreme chunk of the buttons
they thump to change three channels. You know
you're pressing those buggers. There is always
the depthless rheumy yellow of a TV graphic,
a flaring bristle of static as valves crackle and cool.
On quiet roads there is always a chocolate-brown
Austin Allegro lumbering through fog, exhaust
fumes profuse as the breath of a charging bull.
There are always decks of cards, clubs and spades
spreadeagled like rakish lapels. You could kill a man
with that crystal decanter. Glamour and brutality
are held in the span of one hand. Prams are built
like Sherman tanks, folk my age have grandkids
and the whole world really is the colour of those
ochre-tinted photographs in drawers, as if the sun
succumbed to passive smoking, or you're viewing
life through Lucozade cellophane. And so much
gameshow glitz, so much hair. My hotel burns
through a thousand candles per three-day week,
terrible tales about future nostalgia TV stars

were whispered to me by a lachrymose Miss Piggy,
they won't believe we've not been back to the moon
and don't get started on climate change. I have to go—
my laptop is drawing too many quizzical glares
and though barmaids beam wide, in the taprooms
the skinhead gangs and colliers sense something
different about me. You ask how I can linger among
so much drunken driving and heteronormativity
and we will never have an easy answer. All I know
is my train home leaves in an hour and I haven't packed.

Walkback Limit

Within three months the rails will be lifted,
      the visiting officials explained,
priorities in general having shifted
      and motive force transferred to new
networks of roads. Developers will clamour
      for the ticket office, shunting yard
and sidings under the auctioneer's hammer
      and this eternal trackbed, stitched with
seams of foxglove, coltsfoot, celandine, will be coated
      over in tarmac. Tonight the stationmaster
stands astride the granite foundation stone, devoted
      to both progress and commemoration,
two polished patent-leather boots planted
      in opposing centuries. Since he shared
the news, the villagers can no longer take for granted
      the good faith of the men in suits,
whatever Heath might choose today to utter
      about the Common Market, new prosperity,
new buyers for their beef and butter,
      as he readies to despatch
herds of civil servants out to Brussels.
      Closer to home they have already gone
through the motions of parliamentary tussles,
      redemptive amendments to the Bill
thrown out, a rare rebellion by their local Member
      all in vain. All that remains
as the county closes in to this arctic December
      night are the faces now assembling
at the gates, limelit by flights of votive
      oil handlamps repurposed from the stores,

performing a vigil for the final locomotive
        ever to leave the village.
The stationmaster stands to swallow
        the last of the lukewarm tea, sets down
the chipped double-arrow cup; the people follow
        his lead to platform 3 where Rod
grinds a Park Drive dog-end into gravel,
        hoists his body weight up to the cab, flicks
on lights for the passengers boarding to travel
        into the new era. Ella Fitzgerald sings
on the waiting room radio and the freezing
        huddled villagers join in, *we shall not
be moved*, even Basil, voice like the wheezing
        organ he wrestles through Mass
each Sunday morning. From the heavens, lunar
        light drains warmth from the earth
and certain of those present would far sooner
        press ahead and get it over with.
Sensing the mood, the stationmaster calls attention,
        says his piece, evokes the Victorian spirit
of capability which laid the tracks, makes mention
        of the Apollo crew now preparing
to leave for home: we can't know tomorrow's
        world, he reminds the gathering,
but if a man facing darkness borrows
        his noblest predecessors' boldness
then any trial can only make him stronger.
        He glances at the full moon, then his watch,
unsure whether to string the speech out longer
        but the people are already applauding

and the song resumes with greater verve and passion
            and the stationmaster doubts that the timetable
will be adhered to in quite the expected fashion
            given also that the bugler is arriving
only now. His gaze shifts from Orion to Taurus,
            reverts to the knowing full moon;
the villagers add a further verse and chorus
            just like a tree standing by the water side
bridging the elapsing minutes. The bugler is ready
            now. Silence intervenes.
His notes rise, steady
            as the constellations.
The Last Post. Nobody is dying,
            reflects the stationmaster, but clearly
this is bereavement still, the changes denying
            the whole damn place its lifeline,
its permanent way. Some moments of rumination
            pass and Rod starts the engine,
diesel smoke and whistle fill out the station
            and the departure is made.
Brandy and tea are received by the villagers filing
            through the stationmaster's scullery,
who are received by Jean, unflinchingly smiling
            and smoothing her beige polyester dress
and sapped warmth is restored by the tipples
            and the flames that crackle in the grate
and the rueful bonhomie that ripples
            through the rooms like a tentative thaw.
The small television set in the corner is relaying
            flickering pictures from Apollo 17

and the commander, ready to launch, is saying
            as we leave the Moon at Taurus Littrow,
we leave as we come and, God willing,
            as we shall return, with peace and hope
for all mankind. Jean sets about the room refilling
            glasses and teacups and the people
yield with little ado to her twinkling insistence
            and a commentator speaks of the astronauts'
walkback limit, the maximum distance
            they could safely roam from the lunar module
and the stationmaster's thoughts wander
            back to those seven distant weeks of college
and the stationmaster cannot help but ponder
            how it would be had they all used the railway
more—but the time is past for this forlorn mulling.
            His watch says Rod will now be applying
the vacuum brakes and the loco pulling
            in at King's Cross
to be stabled some time later
            up at Finsbury Park depot.
These local losses would facilitate the greater
            good, the visiting officials told him;
high-speed inter-city travel would be approaching
            fast—but tonight, in his small garden,
the metronomic tick of cooling steel is encroaching
            on his thoughts and by second nature
the stationmaster's hand moves again to his pocket
            and the abrupt redundancy of his watch
hits him like a punch. The image of the rocket
            and the men on the moon returns

and the way moonlight is sunlight's reflection
         and the stationmaster crosses a line
and feels the pulse of some grand connection
         to all the unstoried boroughs of making-do
spread tonight beneath the same lunar gleaming,
         to all the middling shires with no rebel song,
no telegenic sheen of heroism redeeming
         their overcast Wednesday endeavours.
The stationmaster has reached his own outer border
         and there is nowhere left to go
but back inside to a kind of holy disorder
         comprising impromptu carol singing,
a game of gin-rummy on the kitchen table
         and Tom the signalman holding court
in the scullery, where railway anecdote and fable
         are dusted down and passed around
a final time: biographies for those never afforded
         posterity, the minor characters
of the branch lines whose minutes go unrecorded.
         Let that preservation group do their best,
thinks the stationmaster, brandy glass uplifted,
         looking out again and no longer immune
to the infectious mood, his gaze now having drifted
         to the stop signal silhouetted by the cold moon.

Diminished

Last night we sang of hedonism and
premodern love, sang for the drinking,
drank for the songs—heroes of the small
hours, vertical survivors, miraculous,
on midnight traffic islands. Take us
to the aftershow, the offy, take us to bed.

The fretboard presses
back against my calloused fingertips,
hard as the whetstone meeting
the knife my dad once gutted haddock with
below an icy running tap, his pleading
knuckles raw as January dawn.

Twenty months before my birth
the Beatles split. Concorde couldn't
stay aloft. Iron, rail, coal and fish:
apologies for former selves.
When I play pop it's either
defiance or denial, I'm not sure which

nor if it matters. Today instead
these wound steel threads must chorus
closed-down foundries. My translucent
plectrum, please. I want to hymn
the world we're in, digital, truncated.
My span contracts. I want to strum

diminished chords all day.
My digits vie for fretboard space,
driven as City traders. How strange
the change from major to diminished.
C diminished, cagey and constrained. A chord
for my generation.

Elegy for Le Grand K

Open the vault
with infinite care,
raise the dome
of polished glass
for a final time:
one false move
may sink satellites,
unravel nanotech.
A century like this
calls for steadiness.

This stolid cylinder
carried the weight
of the world,
casketed regally
against small decay,
its fretful, velvet-
gloved attendants
vexed by the
negligible creep of
discrepancy.

The urge is strong
to place a palm,
absorb the balm
of its assuredness,
allow the gleam
of the Supreme
Kilogram's definitive
iridium to soothe

post-truth disquiet,
smooth out doubt.

Its electromagnetic
successor may not
embody decimal
perfectibility
but twenty atoms
are amiss. Drink
a toast to the K
of precisely one litre,
its desuetude
a subdued *au revoir*
to the palpable.

Railway Time

Seven o'clock is propaganda. Tracks were laid
      and lines were spun. Seven o'clock is
the pure fabrication of markets, the weaving of text,
      standardisation's imperative stamped down
in steel and concrete, in livestock and coal.
      Shunted aside loping into September,
Canterbury hop pickers scrutinise cumulus;
      lightermen look over cargoes of limestone
on yesterday's towpath between Leeds and Liverpool,
      sidelined astride the last lock before dark falls.
This changes everything. Seven o'clock
      is a mass conversion, the chiming of matins,
demand of new deities, timetable's scripture,
      communion of produce of milking shed, abattoir,
crated, containered and set up for sale.
      Synchronisation of whistle, departure:
you step on at Waverley, taking on water
      at Doncaster, eyes to the terminal furlong,
flung along rail by thermal efficiency.
      Couple your pulse to the clatter of wagons,
the pendulum's urge and the surge of stocks:
      seven o'clock is commodification
of basic kinetic compulsions inscribed on
      the trackbed describing the permanent way
of the nervous system, the reach of the network,
      the synapse's firebox spelling propulsion.
This motion becomes a twice-daily transhumance,
      the chant of the axles conducting your heart
and you are the goods being loaded by dockers
      at Felixstowe, you are the item of traffic

they track across zones. An opportunistic
        Silver Street clockmaker labels his wares
to sell 'railway time' and hoodwink your instinct
        to misread the signal, misapprehend moments
not as sensation but measurement. Time is
        against us and time is the zero-sum game
and seven o'clock is consistent branding
        and railway time is committees apportioning
rations of sunshine shipped in from Geneva
        freighting your day with precision anxiety.
Time is imagined and time universal and
        seven o'clock is conjoining the labours
of hands through the junctions from Barrow-in-Furness
        to Dover Priory, Penzance to Thurso
and seven o'clock is surrender and time the
        most finite of all your resources. It's railway
time. This is railway time—and your erstwhile
        looseness is newly relinquished forever,
a central authority's face in each room
        and seven o'clock is the wind through the sidings
that quivers the willowherb, shuts down the branch line,
        that rationalises the parting on platforms
of indiscreet lovers, that passes the motion
        that schedules privatisation of schedules,
sells the last tick of the hour, that sets down
        criteria rating the retail value of
your final reverie on a stopped train as you
        gaze out atop an embankment adjacent
to derelict Derbyshire brickworks, having at
        last felt the moment in perfect and stark

isolation, transcendent in stillness and silence: this
      moment, this moment, this moment this moment
your unscheduled stop outside railway time.

Unsurpassed

They accorded it the honour
of its own Atlantic flightpath,

sparing Ottawa and Galway
the fearsome sonic boom

and the captains used to say
from sixty thousand feet, mach 2

the Boeings cruising far below
seemed to be moving backwards.

A distinctive track to obsolescence,
overtaken only by

events: whereby the leaden pull of
economics outweighs all the

miracles of aeronautic science.
Now witness a stripped fuselage

in Washington or Surrey,
drained of fluid, liveried

in cancellation, confounded
as a carehome patient's

future tense; burnt out
without a mark; yet pristinely

unsurpassed. How we crowd
to coo and mourn

notions of better ways. So it goes.
We knew the trade-off:

pragmatists can't generate
sufficient lift

to counteract the hangaring
of optimism.

Analogue technology,
European harmony;

a week of farewell overflights;
the queen lit up her castle.

Thank you for flying Concorde.
Not all crashes are the same.

The Loudness War is Over

As conflicts go, it was unusual.
Commanders pushed into the red,
annexing airwaves, dancefloor
territory, but none could say
how victory might sound.

Veterans sighed of futility,
the ones who'd glimpsed the void
to apprehend the crushing
finitude of indie rock anthems
that could ever be written.

As their leaders plundered
decibels, civilians remembered
TV dramatisations of a world
without music, a mutually assured
annihilation of dynamics

then one Yuletide exhausted
factions downed algorithms,
remixed carols, kicked a ball
across the no-man's land
beyond audible spectrums.

There was nowhere left to go.
Shell-shocked engineers declared
an armistice, drawing back
the sliders across birdsong
and echoing scorched earth.

Now every clubnight pauses
for the keening of a single
bugle to commemorate lost
nuances. Producers were quietly
upset at how readily you could

move on. This time
it's only rock and roll
but the Loudness War is over
and the world knows how
to come back from the brink.

I saw a pulsing city

I saw a pulsing city driven through
with sweeping boulevards at every turn:
below downtown apartments, out into
the murmur of suburbia, the churn
and clamour of the tumbledown estate
whose visionary planners made a choice
to liberate the traffic of debate,
ensuring every district had a voice

but on each intersection all I saw
were knots of raddled citizens, left mute
and deafened by the dialectic roar
which tore apart the city root by root,
marooned, as if each sidewalk were the shore
on some far, ravaged island of dispute.

Passenger

If there's a patron saint
of passengers, I'm praying now,
temple pressed white to the pane,
lids tight against the pastured squares,
slowed squadrons of cumulus,
church spires, moving water.
None of this is mine,

infrastructure of an age
when some feared suffocation
if folk were shifted
faster than a trot

and to accept the helm,
slant a rudder
into squalling circumstance
is only to surrender the compass
to men of another stripe.

To represent *amen*
I fix on a point
amid diffuse cyans of distance,
conflating sleep and stillness.

The River Don Shipping Forecast

PENISTONE

winter sun strikes Yorkshire stone
bland dazzle on a three-car driveway
townhouses, becoming detached
below the tyre centre's yard
the undisclosed riverbank
falling steadily

WHARNCLIFFE SIDE

safety camera, rooted & inscrutable
overflown by robins
flutter, becoming glide
damp leaf litter flyposts
speed limit signs in mist
50, occasionally 40

HILLSBOROUGH

yawning tram drives head-on into dawn
new sunbeams skewer carriages
liveable, becoming variable
below the flow of Leppings Lane
a single moorhen broods
moderate; loud later

Neepsend

iron railing, rubble, foundations lost
tarmac unrepaired
tracks becoming darker
lurch and flicker of ragwort
in wind and halogen
occasionally eerie

Kelham Island

red lights, real ale
heritage rebirthed
sustainability, becoming hipster
nonchalant in turbulence, a heron
perches on a weir to dip
on balance, good

Wicker

carpet wholesalers, pharmacies
downbeat one-time railway pubs
becoming neon takeaways
between carriageways
saplings shiver, insecure
moderate, edgy later

TINSLEY

Debenhams becoming parking space
becoming tramline, becoming Don
becoming brambled sprawl
a dragonfly surveys the site
dissolves into the glare
veering northeast

MEXBOROUGH

fences swallowed by hogweed
allure of towpath subculture
redundancy, becoming retirement
canal & river locked in a foxtrot
pathside flowerpots set equidistant
poor, fair to good later

RAWCLIFFE BRIDGE

Dutch River perpendicular to drains,
the exit slip to lines of oilseed
sky becoming boundless
a watercourse re-engineered
subsumed as the estuary looms
losing its identity

Three Views of Chapman's Pond

2017

His thumb on the controller yaws the quad.
A clockwise gyre finds herring gulls at rest,
dog walkers on the sea wall, sun-sparked tide,
the Lincoln train's abrupt, slowing blue stroke.

This footage of the water tower's roof
will fascinate the local history group.
They used to say the pond was bottomless.
Developers have padlocked its perimeters.

The drone man cannot hear the whirring servos.
Down Suggitt's Lane a world may yet rotate.

1978

The folklore holds no sway with Mark and Kris:
no phantom horse and cart will glide the brim.
Even so, this stark uncanny half-light.
The captured stickleback mouthing a prayer.

Mark's eyes flare for a tick like a struck match.
Next season they'll have rods and tackle boxes.
They'll land the pike that snapped his uncle's line.
His ankle turns on terracotta fragments.

The two boys dipping nets into the murk.
The sky closing around them like a jar.

1915

The blazing kilns must be extinguished now.
The officer explains that Zeppelins
could navigate upriver by their light.
Walwyn Thomas Chapman exhales pipe smoke.

The boilermen will not refire the steam pump.
The subterranean water leaching in,
unreflective, grey with dust and silt,
will be allowed to rise and brim the pit.

The brick pit between town and sea and sky.
The county's far cusp where dimensions blur.

Homeschooling

It is 2019. You are my son. This is the River Dee.
    We are in Chester, Trump in the White House.
The leaflets displayed on that stand say the Earth
    is flat. Those crackpots are harmless,

the city walls have stood for two millennia.
The drive to south Wales is taking a toll on your mother.
    Six weeks from now we'll learn of the leukaemic myeloblasts
proliferating in her blood and marrow.

I won't know how to tell you the survival rate
    is 35 per cent. Alexa, tell me a joke.
It is 2020 and your mother is discharged
    and there's something

in the air. Six weeks from now we'll all be home
and our attendance to your mother's mother's final breaths
    will be by Facetime. Amid all of this loom
your adolescence, your burgeoning climate anxiety,

a rebel magnolia blossoming
    one week sooner every year. Alexa, tell me
how to respond to a panic attack on the stairwell.
    It is 2021 and the crackpots are attacking

the Capitol building. You are twelve
and ask my permission before saying *what the actual
    fuck?* We don't know how to show the mob
that everything they think and act upon

is wrong, we don't know how to stop them
             storming a ward to wrestle another
mother from her ventilator. I don't know how
             to tell you that the mob

        must be wiped from God's sweet spherical Earth.
It is 2022. The mob is attacking Kyiv
        and this magnolia, bruised brown by late frosts,
will not distract you any longer.

Growing Seasons

How can you bring a child into
this world? Cod landings having dwindled

scant, my dad swapped dockside shifts
for the sorting office's small hours

only for its uncircadian
timesheets to disrupt his heart. Still,

he seeded names to my firstborn.
The lad's now six. He says one day

he'll isolate the DNA
of the immortal jellyfish,

splice its helix with our own
so we'll not die. For now he nurtures

snails uprooted from the yard,
feeds them clumps of sap-steeped weed,

adds eggshell shards for calcium.
His new sibling comes of age

when I'm the other side of sixty.
Cradling both, I point out plants

we seeded amongst clustered frosts
now thrust with tiny tomatoes,

pale green and
foetally clenched.

Scientists say the cod stocks are
replenishing. Scientists say

there are a hundred growing seasons
left in the British soil.

Acknowledgements

Some of the poems in this collection have previously appeared in *Anthropocene, Caught by the River, The Fenland Reed, Fresh, The High Window, Ink Sweat & Tears, The Interpreter's House, Prole, Riggwelter, Route 57, Stand* and *Under The Radar*, and in *DW Cities: Sheffield* (Dostoyevsky Wannabe, 2019) and the Brotherton Poetry Prize Anthology 2019 (Carcanet, 2020). Thanks to all the editors who said yes.

Thanks, too, to Christopher Hamilton-Emery for believing in this book and making it happen. To all the members of the Nunsthorpe Poetry Group for your encouragement and brilliant suggestions. To Robert Etty, Jonathan Kinsman and Jonathan Taylor for close reading and constructive support. To Kate Garrett for horoscopes on the train at midnight.

To the editors of and fellow contributors to the University of Sheffield's *Route 57* journal for accepting me along with the poems, with a particular shout out to Amanda Crawley Jackson, Dan Eltringham and Ágnes Lehóczky for inviting me along to all the cool stuff. To all the Longbarrows for being friends, inspirational poets and world-class drinking buddies. To Brian Lewis for showing the way, and Marianthi Makra for ushering me along it.

Notes

'Every vanishing sparrow leaves Delhi more unliveable': This poem reinterprets, and takes its title from the headline of, a report in the *Hindustan Times* by Shivani Singh, published 20 March 2017, retrieved 5 April 2018 at www.hindustantimes. com/columns/every-vanishing-sparrow-leaves-delhi-more-un-liveable/story-lIf21mobbeiNQ5twuk8j2O.html

'To a Vagrant Black-Throated Thrush Sighted in Grimsby Over Brexit Weekend': In the 2016 referendum on the UK's membership of the European Union, several of the areas voting most strongly to leave were in Lincolnshire. On the day when Brexit was enacted, at the end of January 2020, fireworks were lit in Grimsby to celebrate.

'Dan of the Don': Dan's sculptures can often be seen at the confluence of the River Don and River Sheaf in the centre of Sheffield.

'Ring of Brodgar': The Neolithic village of Skara Brae, around 8km north-west of the Ring of Brodgar, was discovered in 1850 when the earth that entombed it was stripped away by a severe storm. Professional excavation and preservation began in the late 1920s.

'The Old Man of Hoy': The Old Man is a sea stack off the west coast of Hoy island, Orkney. Believed to be little more than 250 years old, it is also expected to collapse into the sea within a few decades.

'Leaving Stromness': Admiral Ludwig von Reuter was

commander of the German High Seas Fleet when it was seized by the British navy at the end of World War I and held at Scapa Flow, Orkney. In June 1919, anticipating that his vessels would be divided up between the victorious Allies, he ordered the scuttling of the entire fleet. Fifty-two of the seventy-four ships sank; some were later salvaged but a number remain on the sea bed today.

'The Pull': Fram was a ship used in three celebrated polar voyages by Norwegian explorers in the late 19th and early 20th centuries. It is preserved at the Fram Museum in Bygdøy, Oslo.

Pulp: In the 2010s, having lost many millions of pounds in central government funding, Sheffield City Council announced that many of its public libraries would either close or pass into the hands of community volunteers. A library in the suburb of Walkley was to be 'saved' by conversion into a café bar, only for the company involved to withdraw late in the day. At the same time a programme of tree felling by the council's private contractor Amey provoked widespread criticism and direct protest action. Many of the trees scheduled for removal were healthy mature specimens, including some planted a century earlier to honour local people killed in action during World War I. The protests eventually brought about a major scaling down of the programme, but not before the loss of many trees and the prosecution of protesters.

'Acton': Hope Gardens is a block of temporary housing built from shipping containers on a 'meanwhile site'—a location earmarked for development but put to another use in the short term. It was assembled in 2017 and scheduled for removal in 2024.

'Walkback Limit': The crew of Apollo 17 were the last people to walk on the moon, bringing to a close the intensive period of human lunar exploration from July 1969 to December 1972.

'Elegy for Le Grand K': 'Le Grand K' is the nickname given to the object used to define the mass of a kilogram from 1889 to 2019. Fabricated from platinum and iridium, and officially named the International Prototype of the Kilogram, it was kept in a secure vault in Paris. It was superseded by a measure based on the Planck constant, a value related to the electromagnetic action of photons and thus hard-wired into the fabric of the universe.

'Railway Time': No standard national time existed in the UK before the mid- to late 19th century, when the publication of railway timetables made it necessary to synchronise the varying local times observed in different localities across the country.

'The Loudness War is Over': The Loudness War is the term given to a period when sound engineers mastered rock and pop recordings with increasingly high audio levels, at the expense of dynamics and overall sound quality. It culminated in the early 21st century.

'The River Don Shipping Forecast': This poem is inspired by images from the photography series *The Shipping Forecast* by

Mark Power (1993–6), exhibited at the Hepworth Gallery, Wakefield, in 2019.

'Three Views of Chapman's Pond': Chapman's Pond is a body of fresh water close to the North Sea coast at Cleethorpes, Lincolnshire, formed from a pit excavated for the manufacture of bricks. Versions of local legend hold that the pond is bottomless, or that the remains of a horse and cart lie on its bed.

'Growing Seasons': The immortal jellyfish (*Turritopsis dohrnii*) is believed to be unique among the animal kingdom for its ability to reverse the ageing process in response to adversity and thus indefinitely avoid death.

This book has been typeset by
SALT PUBLISHING LIMITED
using Sabon, a font designed by Jan Tschichold
for the D. Stempel AG, Linotype and Monotype Foundries.
It is manufactured using Holmen Book Cream 65gsm,
a Forest Stewardship Council™ certified paper from the
Hallsta Paper Mill in Sweden. It was printed and bound
by Clays Limited in Bungay, Suffolk, Great Britain.

CROMER
GREAT BRITAIN
MMXXII